This book
belongs to:

. . . .

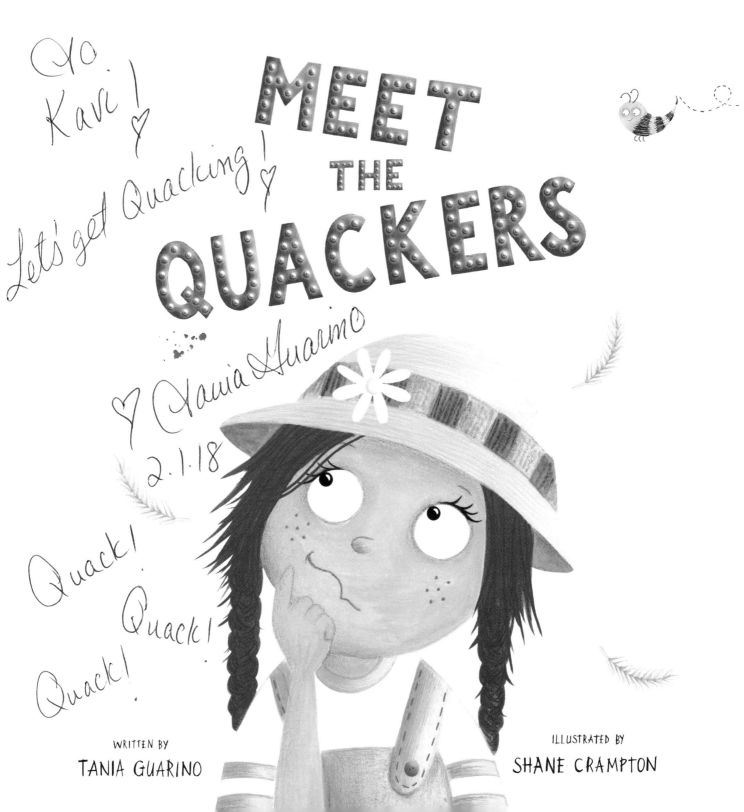

MEET THE QUACKERS

To.
Kavi! ♥
Let's get Quacking! ♥
♥ Tania Guarino
2.1.18

Quack!
Quack! Quack!
Quack!

WRITTEN BY
TANIA GUARINO

ILLUSTRATED BY
SHANE CRAMPTON

Meet the Quackers

Summary: A special delivery of twelve quacking ducklings arrives at the farm and disrupts the routine, peaceful life of the barnyard animals. It's chaos in the barn! Where will they sleep? Will there ever be peace and quiet on the farm again? Kids of all ages will QUACK out loud when reading and counting the Quackers in this fun and lively barnyard counting book! LET'S GET QUACKING!   QUACK! QUACK! QUACK!

Clear Fork Publishing
P.O. Box 870
102 S. Swenson
Stamford, Texas 79553
(325)773-5550
www.clearforkpublishing.com

Printed and Bound in the United States of America.

ISBN - 978-1-946101-29-7
LCN - 2017945974

www.clearforkpublishing.com

To Devin, Chelsea, and Sonny, my own
little Quackers! Never give up on your dreams!

To Jon, for all your support.

To my mother, Fran, for always believing in me.

To Shane, my awesome illustrator, you rock!

And to my Editor, Callie, for loving the Quackers as much as I do!

LET'S GET QUACKING!
WITH LOVE - T.G.

To Cramo (my favourite Viking) for your unwavering
and constant support.

To Jake, Jamie, Flynn, and Spike…for the love and giggles!

To Tania, for trusting me with the Quackers.

Love S.C.

LIVE ANIMALS

Farmer Fran had just finished spreading the hay

when a special delivery arrived.

The barnyard animals gathered 'round for a closer inspection...

"It's a box,"
said Pig.

"A box?"
questioned Horse.

"Yup, it's a
baa-baa-box,"
said Sheep.

"A quite peculiar
box," said Rooster.

"A wiggly jiggly moo-ving box," mooed Cow.

"It's got holes in it," pecked the chickens.

"And letters on the side," said Kitty.

The barnyard friends had no idea what to make of it.

"Our farm has been missing something,"

said Farmer Fran.

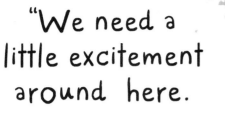

"We need a little excitement around here.

Aww shucks! What we need,"

announced Farmer Fran...

five quacks,
5

6
Six quacks,

"Holy cow!"
said Pig,

7 Seven quacks,

8 eight!

but wait...

Nine quacks, 9   10

ten quacks,

all in a row!

Eleven quacks, 11 twelve quacks! 12

There they go!

Quacking ducklings!

Quack!

Quack!

Quack!

"Farmer Fran,
please send them back!"
begged the animals.

It was chaos in the barn!
The animals were in
a tizzy!

"No fair!
We didn't invite
the Quackers!"

said Cow.

"They're awfully loud!"
neighed Horse.

"Where are they going
to sle-e-ep?"

baa-ed Sheep.

"Oh no you don't,"
    crowed Rooster.

"I rule this roost!

Get along you
little Quackers
and find your
own place to
sleep!"

Quack!

Quack!

Quack!

The chicken house
seemed like a
good place for the
Quackers to bed
down,

but...

The chickens were appalled!

They fluttered about,

flapped their wings

and shook their tail feathers!

"Ain't no one sleepin' here but us chickens!"

clucked the biggest, bossiest chicken of all.

"I don't think so," chewed Horse.

"I'm afraid this is MY stall.

There's only room enough for me...

and that teeny tiny MOUSE!"

The Quackers went BERSERK!

"Don't even
think about it!"
uttered Cow.

 "This spot belongs to me,
so keep moo-ving!"
she said.

The Quackers tried to cozy on in with Sheep and Kitty too,

BUT...

"Uh, uh! Nothin' doin'!" shook Sheep.

"Now skit, scoot, skedaaa-ddle!" he ordered.

"Can't stay here," meowed Kitty twirling about the milk cans.

MILK

Meanwhile...

a keen, sly fox, spying on
the barn smelled his supper
and crept closer,

and closer...

and

CLOSER!

The animals
were in a
flurry!

The Quackers were astounded and bolted through the barnyard door!

QUACK!!!

QUACK!!!

QUACK!!!

"HOORAY!"
clucked the chickens.

"Your quacking
scared the fox away!"

"We are all very grateful,"
said the barnyard
friends.

The Quackers took a
liking to their new
home by the pond.
Everyone was happy.

Peace and quiet at last...

until the delivery truck
showed up!

Tania Guarino lives with her family
in New York's Hudson Valley,
where an abundance of farms and barnyard life are her
constant source of inspiration.
When not writing fun stories for kids, she can be found
riding her bike, gardening, or on the family boat
soaking up the sun and catching fish!
Tania is a contributor to Highlights High Five Magazine.
Meet the Quackers is her first picture book.

visit her online at www.taniaguarino.com

Shane Crampton is a freelance illustrator.
Born and raised in Scotland she now lives in Cornwall,
England with her husband and four sons.
Shane graduated from Falmouth University with a
BA (Hons) Degree in Illustration in 2014.

visit her online at www.shanecrampton.co.uk

CPSIA information can be obtained at www.ICGtesting.com
Printed in the USA
LVIW01n1521110118
562710LV00014B/296

Printed in the USA
CPSIA information can be obtained
at www.ICGtesting.com
LVHW072323270723
753705LV00024B/109